GUITAR SPRINGBOARD by Michae

Harmonic Workout

Simple ways to sound great!

Wise Publications
part of The Music Sales Group
London / New York / Paris / Sydney / Copenhagen / Berlin / Madrid / Tokyo

Published by
Wise Publications
8/9 Frith Street, London, W1D 3JB, England.

Exclusive distributors:
Music Sales Limited
Distribution Centre, Newmarket Road,
Bury St Edmunds, Suffolk, IP33 3YB, England.

Music Sales Pty Limited
120 Rothschild Avenue, Rosebery, NSW 2018, Australia.

Order No. AM984566
ISBN 1-84609-322-8

Translated & edited by Rebecca Taylor.

Printed in the EU.

Your Guarantee of Quality:
As publishers, we strive to produce every book
to the highest commercial standards.

The book has been carefully designed to minimise awkward page turns
and to make playing from it a real pleasure. Particular care has been given
to specifying acid-free, neutral-sized paper made from pulps
which have not been elemental chlorine bleached.

This pulp is from farmed sustainable forests and
was produced with special regard for the environment.

Throughout, the printing and binding have been planned
to ensure a sturdy, attractive publication which should give
years of enjoyment.

If your copy fails to meet our high standards, please inform us
and we will gladly replace it.

www.musicsales.com

Contents

Introduction

Unlike the dry nature of many harmony books, this book allows you to apply the theory you learn as you go along, with hints, tips and detailed song analyses. The basic principles of harmony are presented in an easy and accessible format where you will learn all about simple chords, how to harmonise melodies and how to make your harmonisations as effective as possible.

Once you have reached the end of this book, you will be able to harmonise all kinds of tunes using simple chords and will have a basic understanding of the most important harmonic concepts.

Before we begin, you need to understand the most simple harmonic concept of all—the interval, so let's start by having a look at its definition and see what it means in practice.

What is an interval?

The word 'interval' refers to the space between two notes. Intervals are named according to the number of notes (or 'degrees') they span in a scale, and there are five different types: major, minor, perfect, diminished and augmented. Intervals are always counted from the lower note to the higher one, with the lower note being counted as one.

In this book, we will be exploring intervals up to and including an octave, (intervals larger than an octave are explained in *GUITAR SPRINGBOARD: Advanced Harmonic Workout*).

Unisons, fourths, fifths and octaves

Unisons, fourths, fifths and octaves can be perfect, augmented, or diminished.

- Perfect fourth = five semitones

- Perfect fifth = seven semitones

- Perfect octave = twelve semitones

- A perfect unison occurs between notes of the same name and pitch

In each case, an augmented interval contains one more semitone than a perfect interval and a diminished interval one fewer semitone than the perfect interval.

Seconds, thirds, sixths and sevenths

Seconds, thirds, sixths and sevenths can be major, minor, augmented, or diminished.

- Major second = two semitones, minor second = one semitone

- Major third = four semitones, minor third = three semitones

- Major sixth = nine semitones, minor sixth = eight semitones

- Major seventh = eleven semitones, minor seventh = ten semitones

Tips

- It is really easy to work out intervals on the guitar because each semitone is the equivalent of one fret

- A minor third, therefore, which is made up of three semitones, is equivalent to three frets on the guitar

- If the interval you want to play covers two or more strings, simply count the open string(s) as an additional semitone step and this rule will still work!

The chart below potrays the information on the previous page in a graphic format. This will provide you with a useful reference point if, at any stage during this book, you find you need to remind yourself of the basics.

If you need to work out an interval: start from the note C at the bottom left hand corner of the diagram and move along the horizontal axis until you find the second note of your interval. When you have found the note, trace your finger up the diagram in a perfectly vertical line, and your interval should correspond to the name in the grey box which extends to that point.

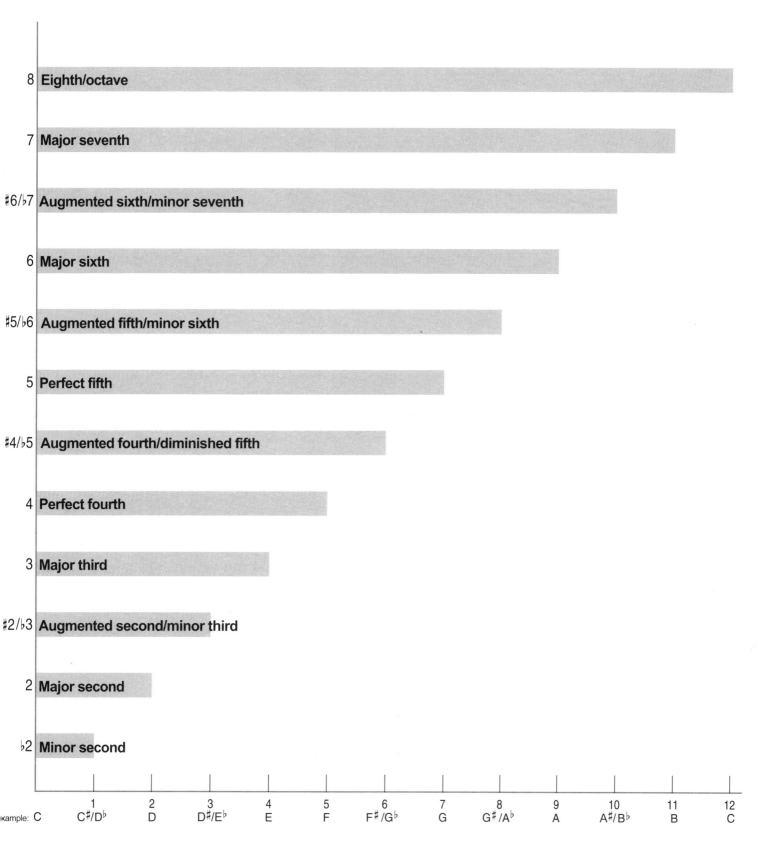

Constructing major scales

A scale consists of eight notes. There are three types of scale: major, harmonic minor and melodic minor. These are explained further in *GUITAR SPRINGBOARD: Scales Made Easy*. Each scale can be divided into two groups of four notes (known as 'tetrachords'). In the major scale, these tetrachords each have the same pattern of intervals, consisting of two whole tone steps and one semitone step.

C major in the first position

The C major scale can be played in the first position using open strings. Specific fingerings need to be learnt in order to play the scale in different keys at a later stage.

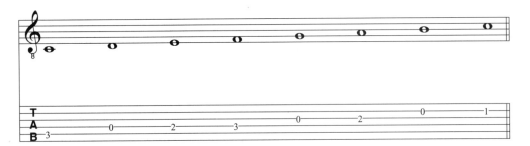

Constructing new scales using tetrachords

All 12 major scales can be easily constructed using tetrachords.

● Use the second tetrachord of C major as the first tetrachord of the new tonality

● Follow this with a new tetrachord with the same interval pattern. Don't forget that the F should be raised a semitone to F♯ in order to preserve the interval pattern and form a semitone step or 'leading note' to G. The new scale is called G major, and its key signature is one sharp

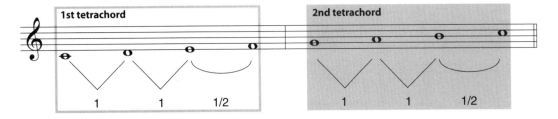

● If the first tetrachord of C major is transposed a fifth lower, it becomes a tetrachord beginning on F

● The B is lowered using the ♭ sign. B♭ thus provides the necessary semitone step up from A. This new key is called F major and its key signature is one flat (☞ page 7)

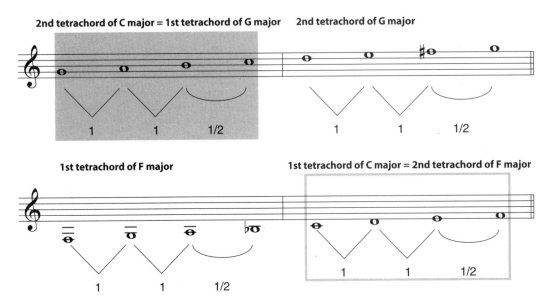

We have seen that tetrachords make it easy to construct new scales. There are 12 keys in total. After C major, which has no key signature, there are six sharp keys and six flat keys. F#/G♭ can be notated either with six sharps or six flats (this is called an enharmonic).

Sharp keys		Flat keys	
G major/E minor	(F#)	F major/D minor	(B♭)
D major/B minor	(F#, C#)	B♭ major/G minor	(B♭, E♭)
A major/F# minor	(F#, C#, G#)	E♭ major/C minor	(B♭, E♭)
E major/C# minor	(F#, C#, G#, D#)	A♭ major/F minor	(B♭, E♭, A♭, D♭)
B major/G# minor	(F#, C#, G#, D#, A#)	D♭ major/B♭ minor	(B♭, E♭, A♭, D♭, G♭)
F# major/D# minor	(F#, C#, G#, D#, A#, E#)	G♭ major/E♭ minor	(B♭, E♭, A♭, D♭, G♭, C♭)

You will notice that every major scale is related to a minor scale by the number of sharps or flats in its key signature. C major is therefore related to A minor (☞ page 15). The chart below shows the different keys and their key signatures. Together, these keys form what we call a 'circle of fifths'.

The circle of fifths is simply a way of graphically portraying the relationships between keys. If we move one step in a clockwise direction, we add one sharp (#) or deduct one flat (♭). Moving one step in an anti-clockwise direction, deducts one sharp or adds one flat to the key signature. This tells us that there is only one note difference between one key and a key one fifth away from it. For example, if we go from C major, which has no sharps or flats, to G major (one sharp), the only difference is that the note F is raised to F#.

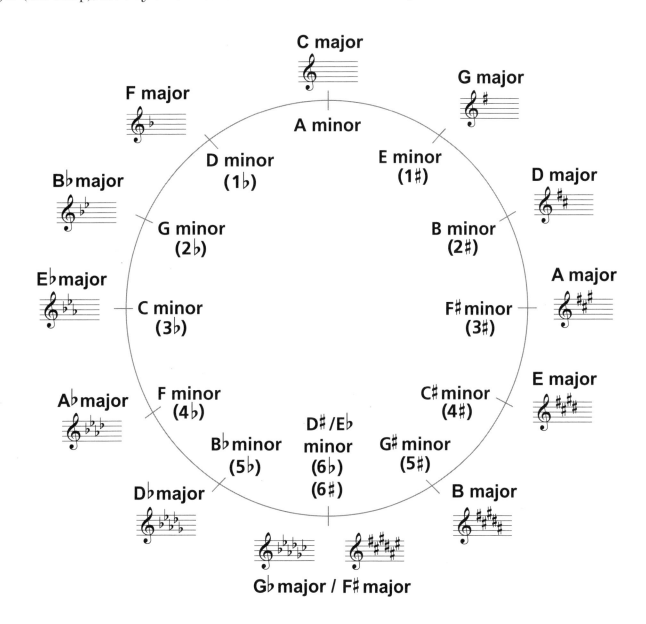

7

Chords

Unlike intervals, which are made up of just two notes, chords are made up of three or more notes chosen in a certain way. Three-note chords are called triads. In its simplest form, the triad is made up of a root, which is the lowest note in the chord, together with a third and fifth above it. The following section will explore the different functions chords can take and will help you apply the theory to real song harmonisations.

Each note of a triad is called a 'voice'. Triads are the simplest form of harmonisation and they appear in four-, five- or six-voice versions (to form more voices, some of the notes can be repeated one or two octaves higher). Due to the nature of the string tunings on a guitar, triads are played in specific forms.

Roman numerals are used to refer to the name of the triad. For example, the triad built on G, scale degree five, is depicted using the roman numeral V. Triads and scale degrees are also known by the names given below.

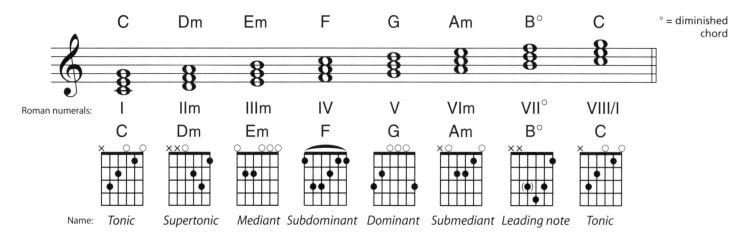

Primary chords

Every key contains primary and secondary chords. Primary chords are those built on scale degrees I, IV and V and are frequently used in cadences (see next page). The major chords C, F and G are the primary chords of C major. The function of these chords is to help define a key—without them tonality is ambiguous.

● C is the tonic (I)

● F is the subdominant (IV)

● G is the dominant (V)

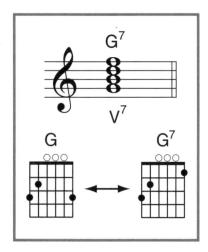

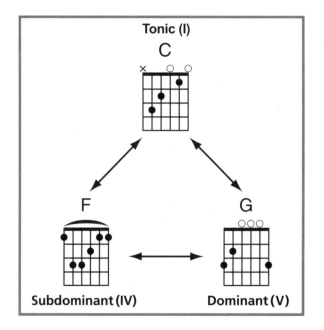

G^7 (above left) is a spcial chord known as a 'dominant seventh'. It consists of four voices and can act as a substitute for B° (VII°). B° (VII°) is strongly related to G (V), but is often substituted with G^7 (extended dominant chord) because it sounds better. G^7 is formed simply by playing the chord B° (VII°) with a G in the bass.

The chords A minor, D minor and E minor are the secondary chords of C major:

- A minor is the relative minor of the tonic (VIm)
- D minor is the relative minor of the subdominant (IIm)
- E minor is the relative minor of the dominant (IIIm)

Tonic (I)		Subdominant (IV)		Dominant (V)	
C	Am	F	Dm	G	Em

Usually, chord changes happen every bar or half bar in 4/4 time—in other words, on the strong beats ('1' and '3'). In 3/4 time the chord typically changes every bar and/or on the third beat. In simple song accompaniments you will notice there are certain sequences of chords ('chord sequences') that appear in all kinds of musical styles.

A cadence is simply a chord sequence that brings a phrase to an end, either in the middle or the end of a composition. Cadences are generally used at points where the music seems to pause, hesitate or stop.

The diagrams below illustrate common cadential sequences using primary and secondary chords.

Common cadences:

- Cadences using primary chords (diagram 1)
- Cadences combining primary and secondary chords (diagram 2)

Chord sequence ·   Cadential formula

1	Chord sequence	Cadential formula
	C → F → C → G/G^7 → C	I → IV → I → V → I
	C → F → G/G^7 → C	I → IV → V → I
	C → G/G^7 → F → C	I → V → IV → I

Chord sequence   Cadential formula

2	Chord sequence	Cadential formula
	C → Am → Dm → G/G^7 → C	I → VI → II → V → I
	C → Dm → F → C	I → II → IV → I
	C → Em → F → G/G^7 → C	I → III → IV → V → I

Harmonising melodies in major keys

The process of adding chords to a melody is known as 'harmonisation'. Each note of the major scale can be harmonised with at least three different triads. The chart below shows some of the more common chords, arranged as a major, a minor and a third possibile harmonisation.

Before you try to harmonise a melody, ask yourself:

- **What key is it in?** (e.g. no key signature = C major or A minor)

- **What is the root note?** (the last note of the melody is often the key note)

Then, make sure you:

- **Analyse the melody** (e.g. look for triads spelled out in the melody: C E G = C major)

- **Try the chords in the chart** (familiarise yourself with the sounds of major/minor chords)

- **Play the chords rhythmically** (e.g. strong beats on the '1' and '3' in 4/4)

Table for the harmonisation of melodies in C major

Chord \ Melody note	C	D	E	F	G	A	B
Major harmonisation	C	G	C	F	G	F	G
Minor harmonisation	Am	Dm	Em	Dm	Em	Am	Em
Third possibility	F	G⁷*	Am	G⁷*	C	Dm	G⁷*

(Each cell contains a guitar chord diagram for the named chord.)

* G^7 is used instead of B°

Tips

- The chords in the table above are a selection of simple accompanimental chords which can be used to harmonise melodies on the guitar. There are many other chords which can also be used, including inversions (☞ page 26) and barré chords in different positions (☞ *GUITAR SPRINGBOARD: Chords For All Occasions*)

- For simple accompaniments it is not important whether the melody note is the root, third or fifth of the accompanying chord. The important thing is the cadence, which should always support and propel the melody

- When practicing, you may find it helpful to construct tables similar to the one above for each of the common guitar keys (C, G, D, A, E, and F majors)

In order to harmonise a melody with a simple accompaniment, you will find that a brief analysis of the songs is useful. Ask yourself:

● What key is the melody in?

● Are there any triads in the melody?

● Which notes come on the strong beats ('1' and '3' in 4/4 time)?

You will also need to ask yourself if any passing notes are being used. Passing notes are a form of melodic decoration. They connect two notes contained within the accompanying chord by stepwise motion and usually occur on 'weak' beats. In the sequence C–D–E–D, for example, the note D would be a passing note because the remaining notes are all part of the C major triad.

The following pages give examples of step by step harmonisation for a selection of songs in C major. First, the song is given as a melody only, and after a brief analysis, the harmonised solution is given.

Melody 1: to be harmonised with simple accompanying chords (first position)

Who Is This Who Enters There? (Melody only)

Traditional

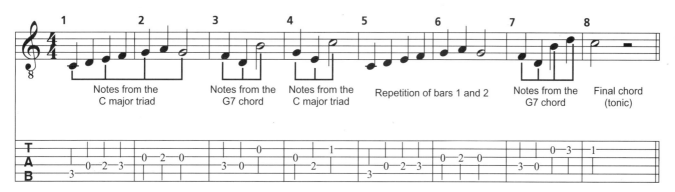

● This song opens with a partial scale beginning on C, rising to the sixth (A). Because the C appears on a strong beat (beat 1) and there are no sharps or flats after the clef, C major is likely to be the tonic chord. The final proof for this is found by looking at the last note of the melody which is also a C

● In the first two bars, C, E and G (which all appear on strong beats) spell out a C major triad. This is a definite sign to harmonise these bars using the C major chord

● In bars 1 and 2, the notes D, F and A are passing notes

● In bar 3 the melody suggests a G^7 chord. Only the root, G, is missing. B^o(VII°), which is also suggested by the melody notes would sound unstable here, because the interval between F and B is a tritone (augmented fourth). If G^7 (root G) is used here, a common bass figuration from tonic to dominant is created (C–G^7/I–V). An ideal solution!

● In bar 4 the C major triad is spelt out in the melody. If we accompany this with a C major chord, our harmonisation so far produces the common cadential sequence: I–V–I

● Bars 5–8 are a repetition of the first four bars with a slight variation in bar 7 and a resolution in bar 9

Analysis

(For the solution ☞ page 12)

Harmonising melodies

Who Is This Who Enters There?

Traditional

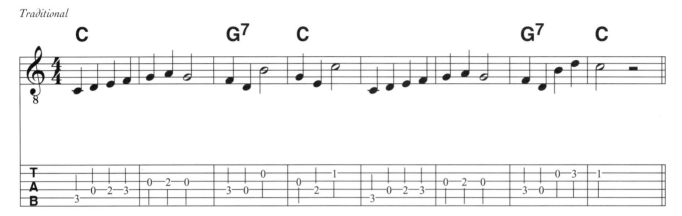

Example 2: to be harmonised with simple accompanying chords (first position)

Auld Lang Syne (Melody)

Traditional

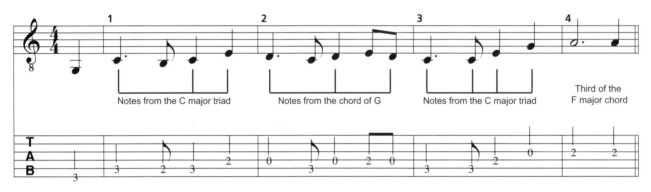

Analysis

- The melody of this song begins with an anacrusis (incomplete bar), G, which has a dominant character. Anacruses are generally not harmonised

- The leap of a fifth to C on the strong beat '1' suggests, as in the previous song, the key of C major. The B in bar 1 (the anacrusis is not counted as a bar) is the leading note of the C major scale and resolves itself on the root note C. The last note of this bar, E, is the third of the C major triad

- In bar 2, the two Ds played between the C and E suggest a G or G^7 harmonisation. In this particular context, G major would sound smoother, since the F of G^7 would clash with the melody note, E, on beat 4

- In bar 3, the C major triad is spelt out in full in the melody, offering the possibilty to complete a I–V–I cadence with C major

- In bar 4, the A is part of the subdominant chord, F major. This passage thus forms a common chord sequence (I–V–I–IV) in the key of C major

(For the solution ☞ page 13)

Auld Lang Syne

Traditional

Example 3: to be harmonised with simple accompanying chords (first position)

Morning Has Broken (Melody only)

Traditional

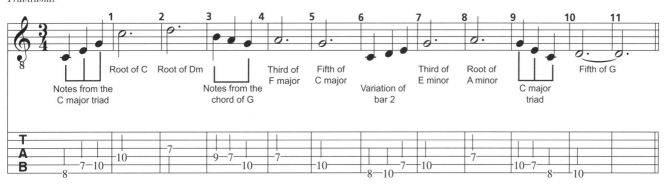

- This song begins with a full bar spelling out the C major triad, which leads to the root note C one octave higher on the strong first beat of the second 3/4 bar. Even though this bar is complete, it still has the character of an anacrusis

- The D, in bar 2 could be accompanied by a G or D minor chord. D minor would make an interesting harmonic change, whereas G would be lighter and rather dull. D minor (II) is also a good preparation for chord V (G) which could follow in the next bar

- The B and G in bar 3 are notes of the G major triad. A is a passing note leading to G.

- In bar 4 the A suggests a subdominant harmonisation. F is chord IV in C major. The only alternative harmonisation, D minor, would be too weak to prepare for the following tonic chord

- Bar 6 is a melodic variation of the anacrusis

- The G in bar 7 could, for variety, be harmonised with an E minor chord. This gives the song a sense of development, and together with an A minor harmonisation in bar 8 creates a strong chord sequence

- The melody in bar 9 is a reverse C major triad

- The D over bars 10–11 offers the possibility of a G major harmonisation. The tied note could also be varied by using Dm in bar 10 and G major in bar 11 forming the sequence II–V

Analysis

(For the solution ☞ page 14)

Harmonising melodies

Morning Has Broken (Harmonised)

Traditional

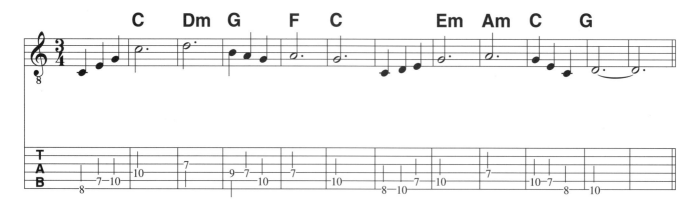

Summary: harmonising melodies

- **Notes of a chord:** always look for notes which form a triad. The presence of a root and third indicate specifically a minor or major chord, whereas a root and fifth together offer the opportunity of either a major or minor harmonisation

- **Passing notes:** these are usually found between two notes of a chord. If there is only one chord note preceding or following the passing note, it is probably more significant than you think! In cases like this, trial and error is the best way to find out what sounds best

- **Semitone steps (diatonic, i.e. part of the scale):** these signify the presence of a) an ensuing subdominant or b)a leading note

- **Melody notes in minor scales:** the three types of minor scale (simple minor, harmonic minor and melodic minor) dramatically increase the possibilities for harmonisation. In analysis therefore, it helps to consider the different options available

- It is wise at first to use chords sparingly, i.e. only on the strong beats (for example in a 4/4 bar only use chords on the first beat or on the first and third beats)

- **Use your ears:** listen to what you are playing. You will produce much better results this way!

- Only when you know what the tonic is can you start to construct cadences

- **Secondary chords:** these can increase your harmonic possibilities, but use them carefully. The more chords you use, the higher the risk of your accompaniment sounding unsettled and rhythmically unstable. The golden rule: less is often more!

We have already seen how each major key is related to a minor key by a common key signature. The term for these related scales are 'relative minor' and 'relative major'. The relative minor scale is built on the sixth degree of the major scale. In C major the sixth degree is A and the simple relative minor of C major is A minor.

The 12 minor keys can be remembered using the simple rule: root of the minor scale = sixth of the relative major scale. Like the major scale, the minor scales can be constructed using tetrachords, following the interval patterns set out below.

The simple minor

There are three types of minor scale: simple, melodic and harmonic. In the simple minor, the semitone steps appear between the second and third notes, and the fifth and sixth notes as follows:

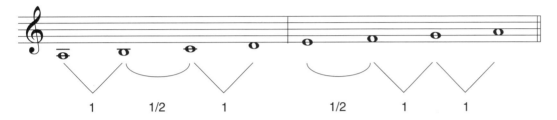

The harmonic minor

The harmonic minor scale differs from the simple minor scale, in that the seventh degree is sharpened. In A minor, therefore, a G♯ takes the place of the G. This forms a leading note, comparable to scale degree VII in major keys, and is harmonised using a major chord.

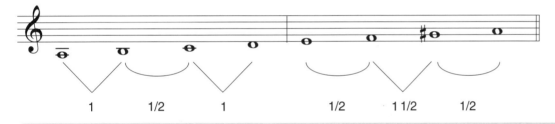

The melodic minor

The third most common minor scale is the melodic minor where both the sixth and seventh steps are sharpened. As a result, this scale is almost identical to the major scale. The only difference between the two is flattened scale degree III in the melodic minor, which leads to a diminished minor chord on scale degree VI.

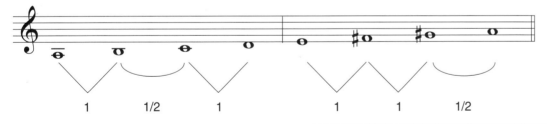

The A minor scale in the first position

On the guitar, the A minor scale can be played in the first position using open strings. Specific fingerings need to be learnt in order to play the scale in different keys at a later stage.

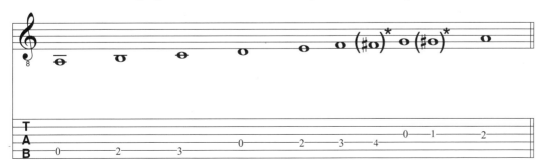

* The G♯ is played in the harmonic minor scale, and the F♯ and G♯ in the melodic minor scale

The simple minor

Minor scales can be harmonised in the same way as major scales, by building up thirds vertically above each degree. In three-part harmonisation, two notes from the scale are placed above the root to produce a three-note chord.

The cadential formula I–IV–V is made up of three minor chords in the simple minor, but these rarely occur together in playing practice. In the place of the minor chord, V, the major chord from the harmonic minor is often used.

In the same way as major keys, the nature of the string tunings on a guitar means that triads are played in specific forms.

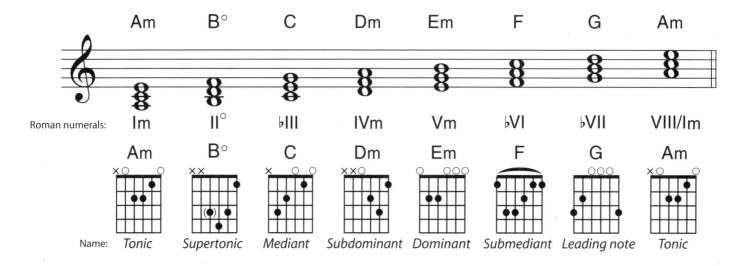

Primary chords

The chords A minor, D minor and E minor are the primary chords of the simple A minor scale:

- A is the tonic (I)
- D is the subdominant (IV)
- E is the dominant (V)

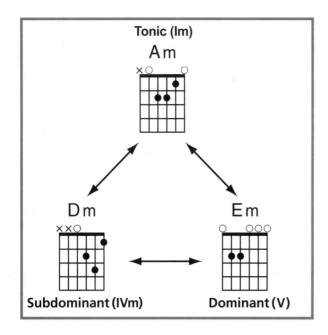

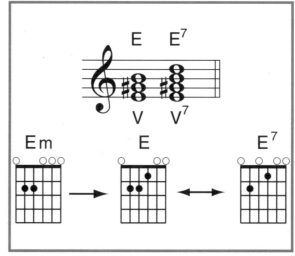

E7 (a four-note chord) can be used in the place of E (V) as a substitute for Em

The chords C major, F major and G major are the secondary chords of the simple A minor scale:

- C is the relative major (III)
- F is the relative subdominant (VI)
- G is the relative dominant (VII)
- B⁰ is the diminished relative subdominant (II⁰)

Tonic (I)	Subdominant (IV)	Dominant (V)
Am → C relative major chord*	Dm → F relative major chord	Em* → G relative major chord
*Extended triad		

* E (V) can be used in the place of Em (☞ page 13)

Cadences

In simple song accompaniments you will come across standard chord sequences (cadences), which are used in all kinds of musical styles. Usually, chord changes happen every bar or half bar in 4/4 time—in other words, on the strong beats ('1' and '3'). In 3/4 time the chord typically changes every bar and/or on the third beat.

As with major keys, cadences are generally used at points where the music seems to pause, hesitate or stop. The diagrams below illustrate common cadential sequences using primary and secondary chords.

Common cadences:

- Primary chords (diagram 1)
- Primary and secondary chords (diagram 2)

Chord sequence / Cadential formula

1

Chord sequence	Cadential formula
Am → Dm → Am → E/E⁷ → Am	Im → IVm → Im → V → Im
Am → Dm → E/E⁷ → Am	Im → IVm → V → Im
Am → E/E⁷ → Dm → Am	Im → V → IVm → Im

2

Chord sequence	Cadential formula
Am → G → F → E/E⁷ → Am	Im → ♭VII → ♭VI → V → Im
Am → F → Dm → Am	Im → ♭VI → IV → Im
Am → G → Dm → E/E⁷ → Am	Im → ♭VII → IVm → V → Im

The harmonic minor

A distinctive feature of the harmonic minor scale is the large interval between the sixth and seventh scale degrees. This interval is a gap of three semitones, otherwise known as an augmented second.

By raising the note G to G♯, the seventh degree has the character of a leading note, similar to the function of scale degree VII in major keys.

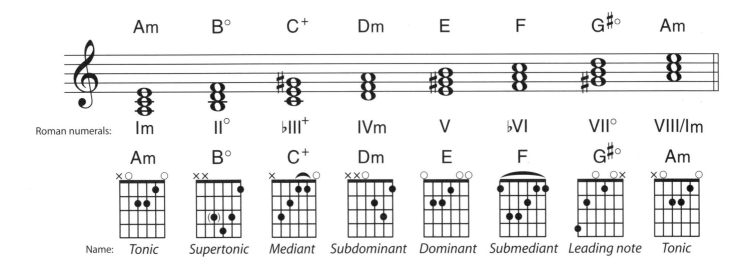

	Am	B°	C+	Dm	E	F	G♯°	Am
Roman numerals:	Im	II°	♭III+	IVm	V	♭VI	VII°	VIII/Im
Name:	Tonic	Supertonic	Mediant	Subdominant	Dominant	Submediant	Leading note	Tonic

Primary chords

The chords A minor, D minor and E major are the primary chords of the A harmonic minor scale:

- Am is the tonic (I)
- Dm is the subdominant (IV)
- E is the dominant (V)

E⁷ (☞ page 16) can be used in the place of E (V).

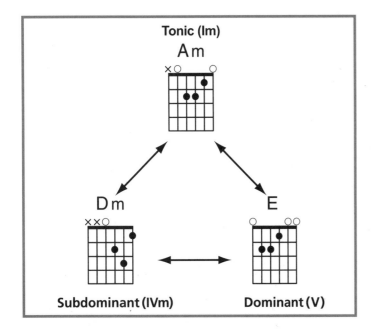

18

Secondary chords

The major chords, C, F and G are the secondary chords of the A harmonic minor scale:

● C is the relative major (III)

● F is the relative subdominant (VI)

● G is the relative dominant (VII)

● B° is the diminished relative subdominant (II°)

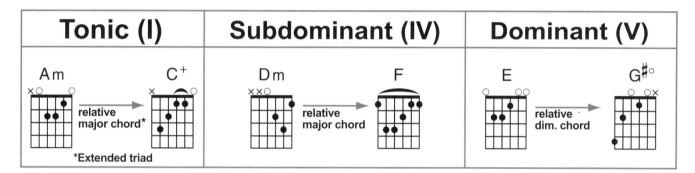

*Extended triad

* E (V) can be used in the place of Em (☞ page 13)

Cadences

The diagrams below illustrate common cadential sequences using primary and secondary chords in the harmonic minor.

Common cadences:

● Primary chords (diagram 1)

● Primary and secondary chords (diagram 2)

Chord sequence   Cadential formula

Am → Dm → Am → E/E^7 → Am	Im → IVm → Im → V → Im
Am → Dm → E/E^7 → Am	Im → IVm → V → Im
Am → E/E^7 → Dm → Am	Im → V → IVm → Im

(diagram 1)

Chord sequence   Cadential formula

Am → F → E/E^7 → G$^{\sharp\circ}$ → Am	Im → ♭VI → V → VII° → Im
Am → F → Dm → Am	Im → ♭VI → IV → Im
Am → Dm → F → E/E^7 → Am	Im → IVm → ♭VI → V → Im

(diagram 2)

The melodic minor

The melodic minor scale is, with the exception of one note, identical to the major scale. The third note of the scale is a minor third away from the root note.

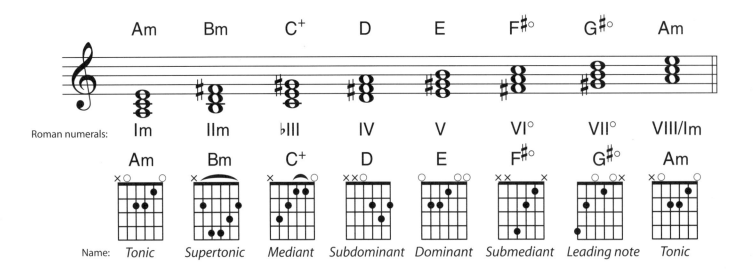

Primary chords

The chords A minor, D major and E major are the primary chords of the A melodic minor scale:

● Am is the tonic (I)

● D is the subdominant (IV)

● E is the dominant (V)

E7 (☞ page 16) can be used in the place of E (V).

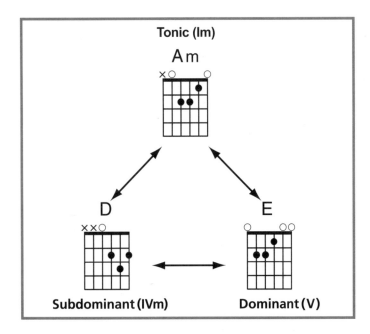

Secondary chords

The chords C major, F major and G major are the secondary chords of the A melodic minor scale:

● C is the relative major (III)

● F is the relative subdominant (VI)

● G is the relative dominant (VII)

● B° is the diminished relative subdominant (II°)

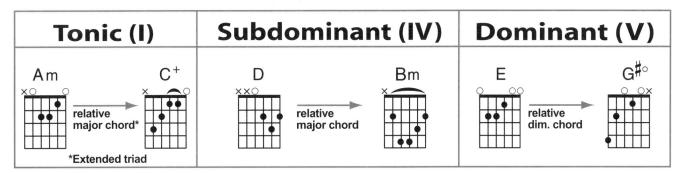

Tonic (I) — Am, C⁺ relative major chord* *Extended triad

Subdominant (IV) — D, Bm relative major chord

Dominant (V) — E, G#° relative dim. chord

* E7 (☞ page 16) can be used as a substitute for E.

Cadences

The diagrams below illustrate common cadential sequences using primary and secondary chords in the melodic minor.

Common cadences:

● Primary chords (diagram 1)

● Primary and secondary chords (diagram 2)

Chord sequence / Cadential formula

1
Am → D → Am → E/E⁷ → Am	Im → IV → Im → V → Im
Am → D → E/E⁷ → Am	Im → IV → V → Im
Am → E/E⁷ → D → Am	Im → V → IV → Im

Chord sequence / Cadential formula

2
Am → D → Bm → E/E⁷ → Am	Im → IV → IIm → V → Im
Am → C⁺ → E/E⁷ → Am	Im → ♭III⁺ → V → Im
Am → G#° → Am → E/E⁷ → Am	Im → VII° → Im → V → Im

Harmonising melodies in minor keys

The following pages give examples of step by step harmonisation for a selection of songs in C major. First, the song is given as a melody only, and after a brief analysis, the harmonised solution is given.

Example 1

Joshua Fought The Battle Of Jericho (Melody)

Traditional

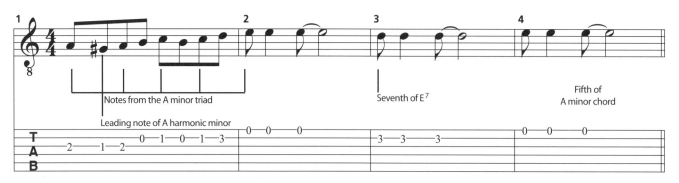

Analysis

- Bars 1 and 2 contain all the notes from the root to the fifth of the A minor scale. Within this passage, the A is reinforced by a leading note, G♯. Therefore the starting note must be the root of A harmonic minor

- In bar 3 the melody note is theoretically the subdominant, which can be harmonised using E7 (D is the seventh of E7). E7 contrasts well with Am

- The E in bar 4 could be harmonised in several ways, but the dominant seventh in the previous bar needs to be resolved and draws the ear towards a tonic harmonisation

Solution

Joshua Fought The Battle Of Jericho

Example 2

The House Of The Rising Sun (Melody)

Traditional

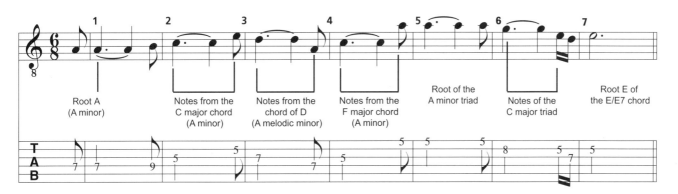

Analysis

- The upbeat and bar 1 of the melody contain the note A which is the root of A minor. The note B which follows can be treated as a passing note between A minor and its relative major chord, C, in bar 2. E is the third of this chord

- The D major chord used to harmonise bar 3 comes from the A melodic minor scale and is more interesting than the dull sounding D minor which could also have been used to accompany this passage

- The C and A in bar 4 (the root and third of A minor) are harmonised with the chord F, because the following bar, which is initially a repetition of the opening phrase one octave higher, can then be harmonised with A minor. In bar 8, the note E suggests a dominant harmonisation (E/E7)

The House Of The Rising Sun

Traditional

Harmonising melodies in minor keys

Every note of the minor scale can be harmonised with chords that are made up from notes within the key concerned. In a similar way to the harmonisation of a major scale (☞ page 10) each note can have several functions (root, third and fifth of the triad, or seventh of a dominant seventh chord). The table below shows a selection of harmonisations for each note.

Rules for harmonising melodies in minor keys:

- Know the key

- Know the tonic

- Analyse the melody

- Try the chords in the chart

- Play the chords rhythmically

Harmonisation of the A minor scale

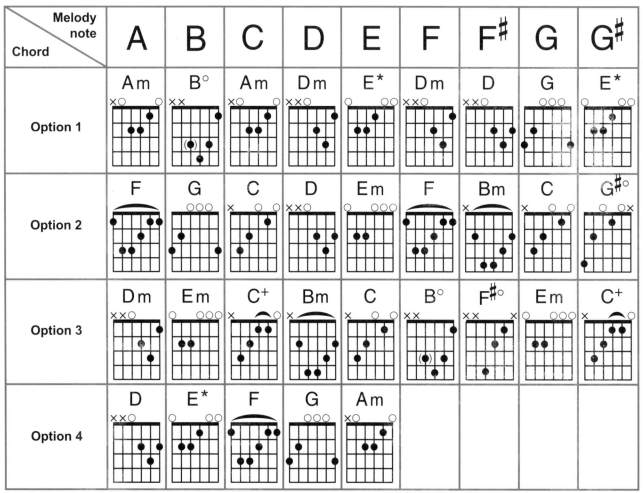

Melody note / Chord	A	B	C	D	E	F	F♯	G	G♯
Option 1	Am	B°	Am	Dm	E*	Dm	D	G	E*
Option 2	F	G	C	D	Em	F	Bm	C	G♯°
Option 3	Dm	Em	C+	Bm	C	B°	F♯°	Em	C+
Option 4	D	E*	F	G	Am				

* E7 can be substituted for E

Tips

- The chords in the table above are simple voicings which can be used to accompany melodies on the guitar. Other chord voicings are also interesting, such as inversions (☞ page 26) and barré chords in different positions (☞ *GUITAR SPRINGBOARD: Chords For All Occasions*)

- For simple accompaniments it is not important whether the melody note is the root, third or fifth of the accompanying chord. The important thing is the cadence, which should always support and propel the melody along

Each chord can be played in several different ways on the guitar. When five- or six-note chords are played, there are three permutations available. These permutations are called 'voicings'. Voicings refer to how the notes of the chord are arranged. To make things easy here, the name of each voicing is taken from the degree of the chord which is in the melody (top) voice:

● Third on top (the highest note is the third of the chord, i.e. E in C major)

● Fifth on top (the highest note is the fifth of the chord, i.e. G in C major)

● Octave on top (the highest note is the key note of the chord, i.e. C in C major)

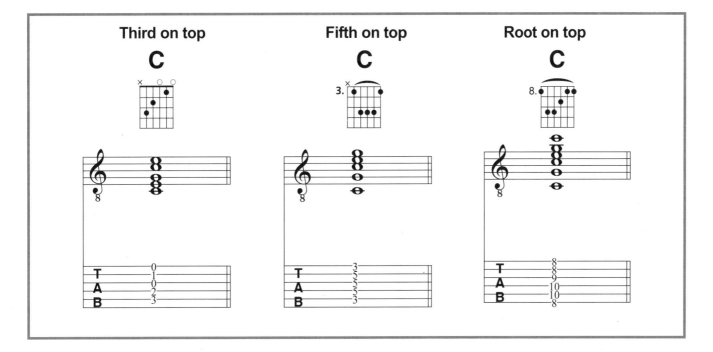

Cadence I–IV–V in A major using five- and six-note chords

In cadences, you will usually find all three of these chord voicings are used. The following example in A major (first position) shows how the three voicings can be put into practice.

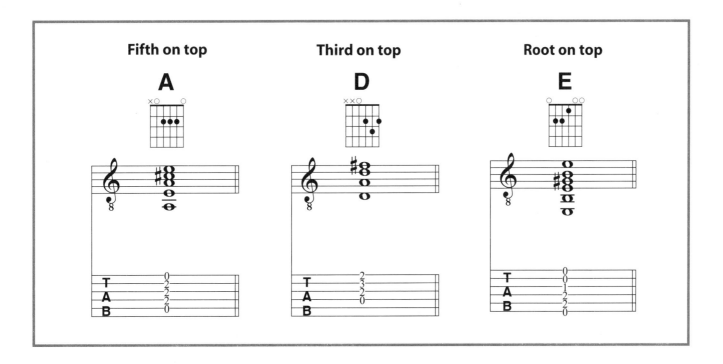

Closed position inversions

So far, we have only encountered triads in root position. By moving the notes of a triad around (inverting the triad), however, every note can act as the lowest note of the chord. In addition to root position there are therefore two possible inversions of a triad which are simply labelled as first and second inversion. These extend the possibilities for harmonisation.

If the notes of the triad are within an octave of each other, it is called closed position. The diagram below shows the inversion of a C major triad in closed position.

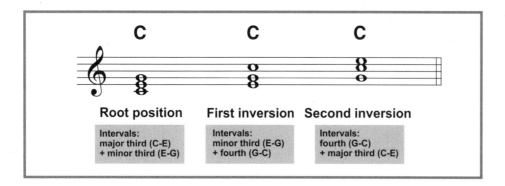

Root position	First inversion	Second inversion
Intervals: major third (C-E) + minor third (E-G)	Intervals: minor third (E-G) + fourth (G-C)	Intervals: fourth (G-C) + major third (C-E)

The three notes of a closed position triad can be constructed as follows:

● On the G, B and E strings

● On the D, G and B strings

● On the A, D and G strings

● On the E, A and D strings

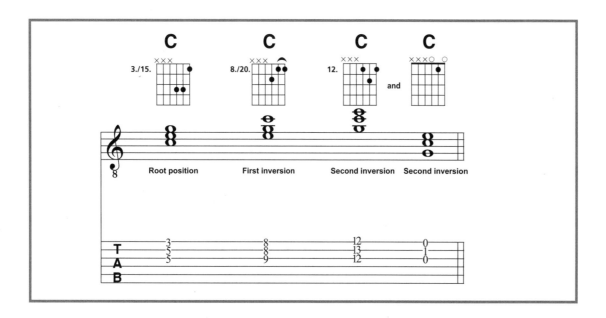

Tips

● To help you get to grips with inverting triads, you may find it useful to write out all the inversions of three-part chords in closed position as in the diagram above. Practise these chords on the guitar in the common keys of C, G, D, A, E and F majors, as well as the minor keys

● Playing three-note chords with the plectrum requires some practice. Strumming three strings with up- and down-strokes without playing the strings which are not being used is quite tricky to master! (☞ *GUITAR SPRINGBOARD: Technical Workout*).

26

In chord sequences, inversions of three-note chords are usually played in particular patterns. A good example is the cadence I–IV–V (C–F–G):

● Root position (I) – second inversion (IV) – first inversion (V) – root position (I)

● First inversion (I) – root position (IV) – second inversion (V) – root position (I)

● Second inversion (I) – first inversion (IV) – root position (V) – root position (I)

Cadence I–IV–V in C major using three-note triads

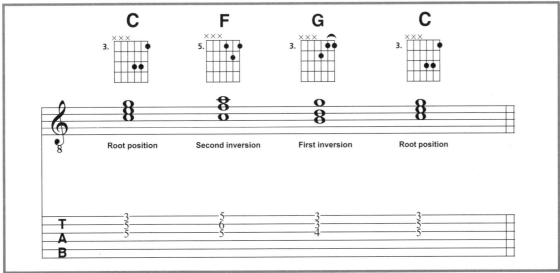

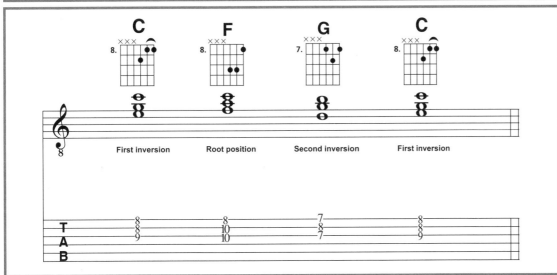

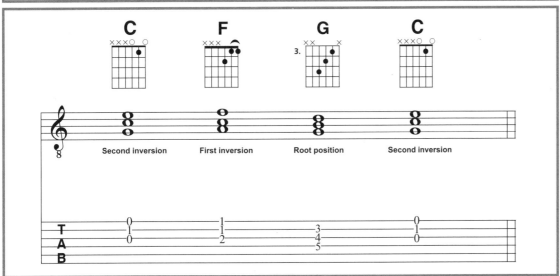

Open position inversions

When the notes within a triad span more than an octave, the triad is said to be in open position. It is easy to play open position triads—simply play the middle note of the triad one octave lower than its original pitch.

The diagram below shows the inversion of a C major triad in open position.

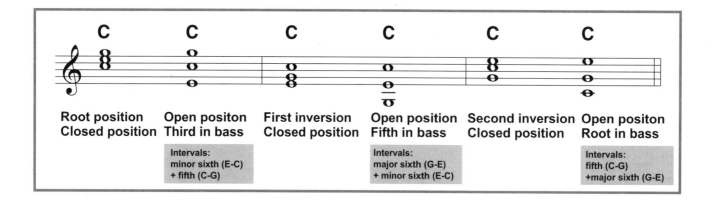

Root position Closed position	Open positon Third in bass	First inversion Closed position	Open position Fifth in bass	Second inversion Closed position	Open positon Root in bass
	Intervals: minor sixth (E-C) + fifth (C-G)		Intervals: major sixth (G-E) + minor sixth (E-C)		Intervals: fifth (C-G) +major sixth (G-E)

On the guitar the three notes of an open position triad can be played using the following string combinations. The diagram below shows these in practice.

- A, G and B strings

- E, D and G strings

- D, G and E strings

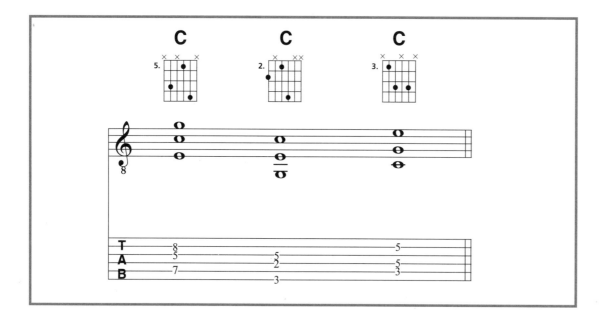

Tips

- You might find open position slightly tricky to master if you are using a plectrum. It is important that any open strings are well dampened with the fretted hand. You can do this by using a slightly angular finger position, by which the fingers of your fretted hand gently touch and thus dampen the open strings

- In the same way as closed position triads, writing out all inversions in open position and their subsequent practise on the guitar is highly recommended

Open and closed position chords in practice

In a similar way to the simple harmonisation of a melody with chords using more than three strings (☞ page 8), a melody can also be harmonised with three-note chords. In this instance, the melody is on top, and below it are various open and closed position triads.

Study the next song *Morning Has Broken* carefully to see how open and closed position triads are used. The melody is on page 13.

Harmonisation using three-note chords in open and closed position

Morning Has Broken

Traditional
Arr.: Michael Morenga

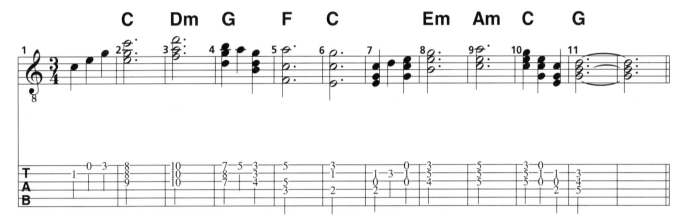

Analysis

- Bar 1 is an introductory passage, which, in this instance, should not be harmonised

- Bar 2: first inversion C major triad. C is the melody note, the next note below the C is the fifth, G

- Bar 3: first inversion D minor triad. D is the melody note, the A the fifth and F the third of D minor

- Bar 4: two of the melody notes (B and G) are contained within the G major triad. In order to emphasise the melody here, the note A is treated as a passing note and therefore is not harmonised

- Bar 5: the F major harmonisation here is in open position which makes the chord sound more consonant

- Bar 6: by using another open position triad, the C major chord also sounds very consonant, even though the third is in the bass. Normally, a third in the bass would sound unstable and demand resolution

- Bar 7: once again the melody contains two notes from the chord of C major. Here, the first and second inversions are used. The D is left unharmonised as it is a passing note

- Bar 8: the note G fits to an E minor chord in second inversion

- Bar 9: A is the root of the A minor chord, which appears here in first inversion

- Bar 10: the descending melody contains all three notes of the C major triad

- Bar 11: the note D is the fifth of the G major triad in root position

Voice leading

Voice leading refers simply to the continuity between successive notes. For example, when moving from a root position C major triad played C–E–G to an F major triad in second inversion, played C–F–A, you might say that the middle voice rises from E to F while the top voice rises from G to A. Instead of thinking of the two successive chords vertically as separate, voice leading concentrates on the linear continuity between notes.

Successful voice leading on the guitar requires specific techniques. The well-known phrase 'keep each voice independent and avoid parallel fifths', traditionally practised in classical theory and most piano music, does not always apply to voice leading on the guitar. In fact, parallel fifths are trademarks of much guitar music (☞ Power chords, *FIT FOR GUITAR: Advanced Harmonic Workout*). The three most important things to remember are:

● Notes common to both chords should be left at the same pitch

● Always move from one chord to the next using the smallest possible steps (semitone or tone)

● The bass should move in contrary motion to the other chord voices. If the bass rises, the chord voices should fall; if the bass falls, the chord voices should rise

Voice leading using four-note chords

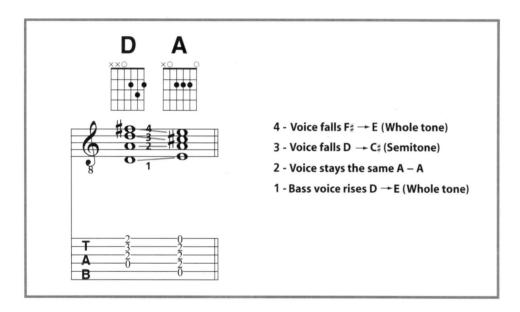

4 - Voice falls F♯ → E (Whole tone)

3 - Voice falls D → C♯ (Semitone)

2 - Voice stays the same A – A

1 - Bass voice rises D → E (Whole tone)

Voice leading using five- and six-note chords

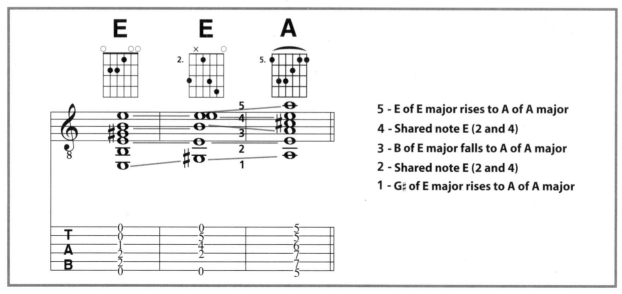

5 - E of E major rises to A of A major

4 - Shared note E (2 and 4)

3 - B of E major falls to A of A major

2 - Shared note E (2 and 4)

1 - G♯ of E major rises to A of A major

Multi-voice chords in practice

There are several useful ways of adding interesting tone-colour to an accompaniment.

● Three-note chords can be extended by doubling different notes, meaning that they can be played in many forms on the guitar

● Barré chords (☞ *GUITAR SPRINGBOARD: Chords For All Occasions*), are well suited to rhythm guitar

● The use of open strings in chord shapes, to which the keys D major, A major and E major are most suited, has its charm (☞ Playing with open strings, *GUITAR SPRINGBOARD: Advanced Harmonic Workout*)

The following examples show two common chord sequences and their voice leading patterns.

Sequence using multi-voice chords in D major. Descending bass line

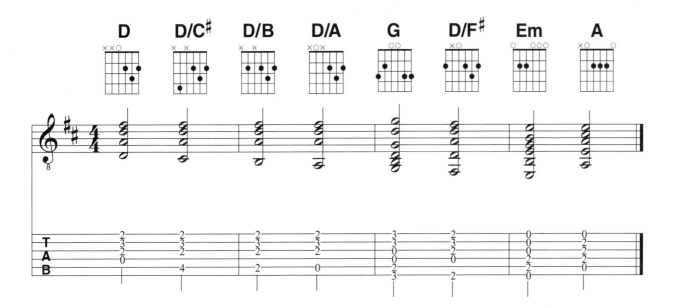

Sequence using multi-voice chords in C major. Descending melody line

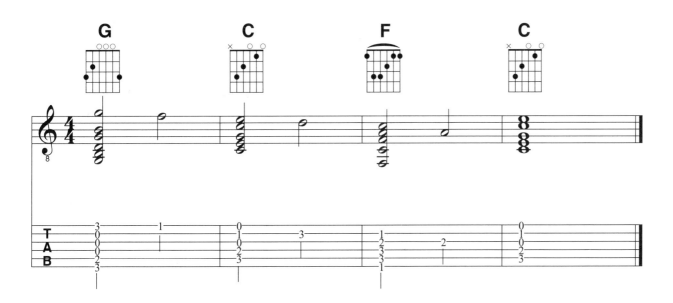

31

Summary

- **Triads:** in the major scale and the three types of minor scale (simple minor, harmonic minor, melodic minor) there are four types of triad
- **Simple four-note chords:** usually take the form of a dominant seventh chord, which can be used as a substitute for the dominant triad
- **Interval structure:** the intervals are labelled as follows: 1 = root, $\flat 3$ = minor third, 3 = major third, $\flat 5$ = diminished fifth, 5 = perfect fifth, $+5/\sharp 5$ = augmented fifth
- **Occurence of triad in major/minor scales:** known as 'scale degrees' in the respective scales

The following table gives a brief overview of the chord types you have learnt so far. Each chord is explained in terms of its interval structure and on which scale degrees it occurs in major and minor keys.

Chord type	Interval structure	Occurrence of chord type in major keys	Occurrence of chord type in minor keys
Major	1 3 5	I, IV, V	$\flat$III, V, $\flat$VI
Minor	1 $\flat$3 5	IIm, IIIm, VIm	Im, IIm, IVm, Vm
Diminished	1 $\flat$3 $\flat$5	VII°	II°, VI°, VII°
Augmented	1 3 $\sharp$5	-	$\flat$III^{+}
Dominant seventh	1 3 5 $\flat$7	V^{7}	V^{7}

What next?

Once you have mastered the techniques in this book, you are ready to progress to *GUITAR SPRINGBOARD: Advanced Harmonic Workout* where you can learn about:

- Barré chords
- Extended triads: sus2, sus4, sixths, ninths, power chords and slash chords
- Four part harmony
- Adapting chords for five voices
- Mediants: modulating using mediants
- Modal interchange
- Secondary dominants
- The diminished seventh chord